Maureen —
only you could
appreciate the humor
in this little
book!!

Hope you are feeling
better soon!

Love
Cathy

50

DAYS

WORSE THAN YOURS

50 Jobs Worse Than Yours
50 Relatives Worse Than Yours
50 Boyfriends Worse Than Yours

50 DAYS

WORSE THAN YOURS

Justin Racz

with Alec Brownstein

BLOOMSBURY

Published by Bloomsbury USA, New York
Distributed to the trade by Holtzbrinck Publishers

All papers used by Bloomsbury USA are natural, recyclable products made from wood
grown in well-managed forests. The manufacturing processes conform to the environmental
regulations of the country of origin.

Library of Congress Cataloging-in-Publication Data has been applied for.

ISBN 1-59691- 263-4
ISBN-13 978-1-59691-263-2

First U.S. Edition 2006

1 3 5 7 9 10 8 6 4 2

Designed by Justin Racz and Elizabeth Van Itallie
Printed in Singapore by Tien Wah Press

For our mothers, Ellen and Judy.

Contents

25. Pimple on Prom Night
26. Forgot Permission Slip
27. Saturday at the Water Park
28. Gas Hits $3.19/Gallon
29. Latte Hits $3.69/Grande
30. Suntan 360°
31. Team-Building Field Trip
32. When Pigeons Attack
33. Wheelie Gone Awry
34. Ricky Gets Atomic Wedgie
35. Twenty-one Years and One Day Old
36. Ate Bad Oyster
37. Bad Break
38. New BB Gun
39. Not Enough Snow for a Snow Day
40. Flu, Day 5
41. Mailed Priceless Stamp
42. Buried
43. Mayday, Mayday!
44. Ran with the Bulls
45. First Day Back at the Gym
46. Rabies Vaccination Day
47. Nonagenarian Renews Driver's License
48. Fastball in the Nuts
49. Thanksgiving at the In-laws'
50. Your Last Day
51. Your Day

1. Adam and Eve Eat Apple

THE DAY

According to Genesis, Eve wanders from Adam and is tempted by Lucifer, in the form of a serpent, who seduces Eve into tasting the forbidden fruit from the Tree of Knowledge.

WHO SAW

God.

BENEFIT

It was delicious.

DRAWBACK

Only expulsion from Eden, original sin, mortality—no big deal.

LESSON

When God says don't eat, don't eat.

FUN FACT

Death is the mother of all beauty. So we've got that going for us, which is nice.

2. Bris

THE DAY

Let's face it, any day involving genitalia and a scalpel is a bad day, especially when it's your little willy under the knife.

HAZARD

A slip of the wrist.

WHO SAW

As you lie naked and squirming, you're surrounded by everyone in your family, friends, well-wishers, business associates, and caterers, all of whom brought cameras.

DURATION

Two bites of a bagel.

BENEFIT

Your nerve endings are not completely formed yet.

DRAWBACK

Strange bearded man cuts off the tip of your Johnson.

3. Hunting with Cheney

THE DAY

A fun-filled day with your Halliburton cronies spent smoking cigars, drinking brandy, hunting quail, and getting shot in the face by the vice president.

DURATION

Two months, if you count time in the ICU and all the interviews during the ensuing media frenzy.

WHO SAW

Luckily, the other members of the hunting party. Otherwise Cheney would have buried you in the middle of the field while you were still breathing.

COMMUTE

Air Force 2.

BENEFIT

More military contracts than you can shake a stick at.

DRAWBACK

Might not get invited to Karl Rove's birthday party at the pistol range.

4. SATs

THE DAY

Nothing big. Only an exam that will determine your success in life.

HAZARD

If you score poorly, you'll end up working as the assistant night manager at Denny's.

BENEFIT

The assistant night manager at Denny's likely gets a discount on the Moons Over My Hammy breakfast.

DRAWBACK

The kid sitting next to you during the test has a runny nose, the sniffles, and whooping cough.

LESSON

If you have to guess, don't guess E.

FUN FACT

On the 2006 College Board SAT, 4,411 students received miscalculated low scores—one test was off by as much as 450 points on the 2,400-point exam—due to excessive moisture that caused the answer sheets to expand before they were scanned. (And some thought the test's cultural bias was a concern . . .)

5. Stranded at the Airport

THE DAY

You arrive two hours early, your flight is delayed twenty hours, you spend the night on the tiles outside the Taco Bell Express in Terminal D.

DURATION

Could be hours. Could be days.

DAMAGE

Splitting headache. The Hare Krishnas at Gate 26B have been jammin' for the past six hours.

BENEFIT

Day-old Cinnabons in Terminal A are half price after five o'clock.

DRAWBACK

The guy sleeping next to you has night terrors.

LESSON

Next time, pack your prescription drugs in your *carry-on* luggage.

6. Saturday A.M. Violin Practice

THE DAY

Every Saturday morning, from six to eleven. Sunny, cloudy, rainy, snowy—it doesn't matter.

DURATION

Until you get it right!

BENEFIT

It's never too early to start rounding out your college applications.

DRAWBACK

Having to drown out the sounds of friends frolicking in the streets by playing extra loud.

TRAUMA

Chin calluses.

LESSON

Suzuki Violin Exercises, volumes 1–12. Know them well.

7. Shark Bite

THE DAY

Just another day of Air Guard search and rescue training, except this soldier found something he wasn't looking for—a great white.

LOCATION

In between rows two and three of the shark's teeth.

BENEFIT

It beats those brutally hot Iraq summers.

DRAWBACK

Can never watch *Jaws* again without crying. Or your favorite *Jabberjaw* cartoons.

LESSON

Choose KP duty. There's no glory in peeling potatoes, but you don't lose a leg, either.

FUN FACT

An HH-60G Pave Hawk helicopter is equipped with a rescue hoist with a 600-pound lift capability. A great white shark weighs up to 4,500 pounds. Shark wins. You lose.

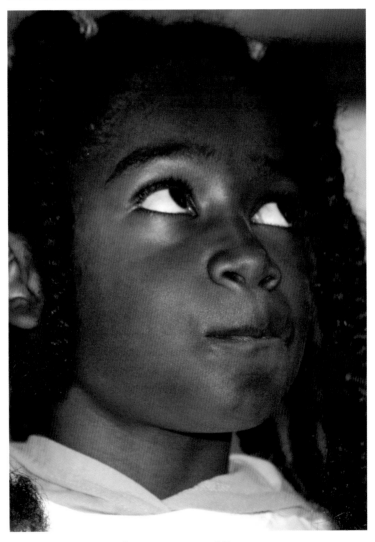

8. Lost the Spelling Bee

THE DAY

"Centrifugal," "sarsaparilla," "mucilaginous." Those she was ready for. But when "mycetismus" was called— despite knowing its country of origin, and hearing the word repeated four times—the Bee inserted its stinger.

WHO SAW

Only the Scripps National Spelling Bee judges and the nation watching from home.

DAMAGE

Deep, lasting emotional scarring.

BENEFIT

There's no trophy for second place. There is a ribbon though.

DRAWBACK

Everyone back home calls you an L-O-S-E-R.

LESSON

It's never too early to be introduced to disappointment.

9. Ran Out of Ketchup

THE DAY

You grilled your burger to perfection and toasted up some crispy "freedom" fries. You have an ice-cold Pepsi to wash it down. But you may as well throw it all in the trash, because some jackass put an empty ketchup bottle back into the fridge, and that jackass is you.

TRAUMA

Sprained wrist from squeezing and pounding on the bottle trying to extract the last precious dollop.

LOCATION

Precisely 4.3 miles from the nearest ketchup purveyor.

BENEFIT

The average meal consisting of a burger and fries is 980 calories. You just saved yourself an hour and a half on the treadmill.

DRAWBACK

You're freaking starving.

LESSON

In Belgium, they put mayonnaise on their french fries. Gross.

10. Bridesmaid, Yet Again

THE DAY

The tenth time—and the last! No more starving to fit into ugly dresses. No more buying pre-wedding gifts, writing fake, witty toasts, and pretending to be happy that someone you never even liked in the first place found her "soul mate."

THE LOOK

$600 disposable sickly pink dress, matching shoes, and a grim smile.

THE COST

The price of being a good friend, $2,350 with airfare and hotel.

DURATION

Wait until the band plays "Shout!" for the third time, and then you're officially allowed to leave.

BENEFIT

Getting yet another silver key chain bridesmaid gift.

DRAWBACK

Nobody looks good in pink taffeta. *And* you're out $600.

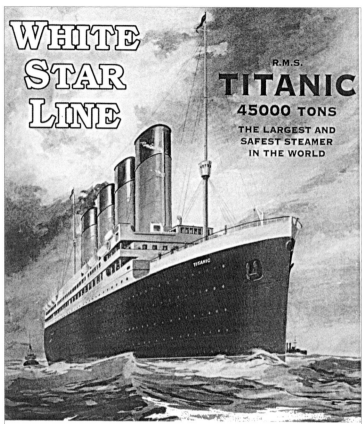

11. Bought *Titanic* tickets

THE DAY

March 3, 1912, five weeks before sailing on April 10, 1:55 p.m.

THE COST

£660 ($3,330 American) for a two-bedroom parlor suite; £86 ($430) for a single first-class ticket; £7 ($35) for a third-class ticket.

BENEFIT

Seven pounds for a luxury cruise seemed like a good deal at the time.

DRAWBACK

It was not.

LESSON

Caveat emptor. Voyages on ridiculously enormous passenger crafts have historically gone badly, such as Howard Hughes's Spruce Goose and the zeppelin *Hindenburg*. When commuter flights to outer space become available, think twice.

FUN FACT

Third-class ticket holders were sealed off from the other classes. When they emerged on deck, all the lifeboats were gone.

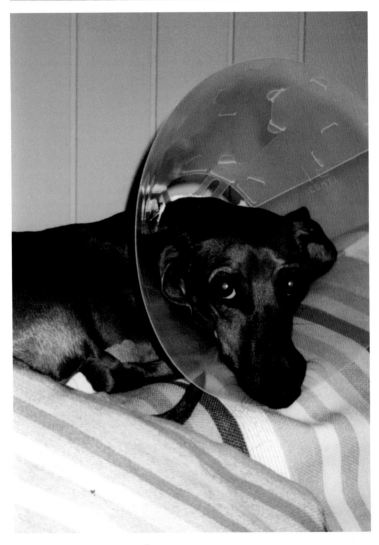

12. Not This Dog's Day

THE DAY

Spot just didn't see that van coming.

DURATION

Two hours! He had to wait behind a horse, a monkey, and a snake.

BENEFIT

A pet's unconditional love in the form of licks and kisses has been proven to increase its owner's longevity.

DRAWBACK

One reason humans have jobs is to get health coverage. But dogs don't work. So when they sprain an ankle, who foots the bill? You do.

FUN FACT

One can never put a price on a pet—except in Beijing, where you can order a hot dish called Dog Five Ways.

LESSON

Leash the bitch.

13. Birthmas

THE DAY

You had the misfortune to be born on December 25, thereby combining the two biggest gift-receiving days of the year into one. And if you think you're going to get two presents from everyone, you're sadly mistaken.

MEALS

Even if you're a vegetarian, it's Christmas ham.

TRAUMA

One year, you got two lumps of coal: one for Christmas and one for your birthday.

BENEFIT

People won't forget what day your birthday is.

DRAWBACK

Though it may be *your* birthday, it's also Jesus' big day. And you can't go head-to-head with JC.

LESSON

Santa is in the business of delivering Christmas presents, NOT birthday presents.

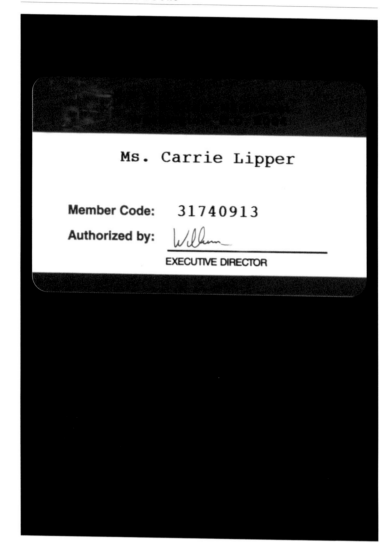

Ms. Carrie Lipper

Member Code: 31740913

Authorized by:

EXECUTIVE DIRECTOR

14. AARP Card Arrives

THE DAY

It's the day you learn you're officially old.

HAZARD

What's next? The Hip Replacement Newsletter?

FUN FACT

Social Security kicks in when you're sixty-seven. So what? It's not like there's going to be any left by then.

BENEFIT

Members get a free subscription to *AARP The Magazine*. Look, it's Susan Sarandon on the cover, as if to say "See, 50 isn't fatal! She looks great!"

DRAWBACK

Seniors save $8 at Anheuser-Busch Adventure Parks SeaWorld and Busch Gardens! But only on "Terrific Tuesdays."

LESSON

"Rage, rage against the dying of the light!"
—Dylan Thomas

15. Jury Duty

THE DAY

Jurors from the O. J. Simpson trial got million-dollar book deals and were interviewed on Larry King. You get to spend eight hours listening to experts testify on the potentially adverse effects of exposure to chalk dust in the workplace.

LOCATION

The twelve-by-eight-foot jury box is your new home.

WHO SEES

The defendant. And if you're on the jury of a Mafia trial, you might want to start your car by remote for a few months.

DURATION

Every surprise witness adds a day to the trial.

BENEFIT

The catered lunch from the local deli is free.

DRAWBACK

There are rarely sexy or exciting revelations in the courtroom. *Law & Order* lied to you!

16. Getting Whacked

THE DAY

Rocky enjoyed his last Gino's Parmesan hero before being taken out back and disposed of.

DURATION

Plastic and bones can be compacted in a minute.

LOCATION

A mile from the Fresh Kills landfill in Staten Island, New York. A slightly more fashionable address than Sleeping with the Fishes, New York.

BENEFIT

A Mafia soldier's wife will be compensated for her most unfortunate loss. Crime families might kill their own, but wives are taken care of.

DRAWBACK

You'll never make capo.

LESSON

Crime pays. Pretty well actually, just not for long.

17. Ousted from Clique

THE DAY

Yesterday, Jacqueline Lane, a member of the Hot Five, was doing the middle school catwalk down the hallway. The next day? She's banished like Eve from Eden all because she let Nate Taylor go to second, *over* the sweater. But at the start of the year, the Five had agreed that all hookups beyond first base must be negotiated among the group. Jacqueline's unilateral decision to hook up with a NAH (Not a Hottie) gave the Five a permanent black eye. There was nothing they could have done. Jacqui had to go.

DURATION

She went from Hot to Not in all of five minutes.

LOCATION

It went down like this: After Jacqui got dropped off by her Mom—B.T.W., *so* uncool—she went to meet the Five in the alley. No one there. But as she headed toward Earth Science class, the girls slapped her books to the ground and called her an [unprintable] skankbag.

WHO SAW

Like, *everyone*!

BENEFIT

Well, at least she *has* a second base.

DRAWBACK

Eating with the weirdos from math league. Measuring the surface area of a Jell-O cube is NOT cool.

18. Valentine-less Day

THE DAY

A stupid Hallmark holiday where stupid people buy stupid flowers and go out to stupid romantic restaurants. It's stupid. But you're not bitter you spent it by yourself watching *Mama's Family* reruns on TV Land.

LOCATION

Your couch.

HAZARD

Breaking down and calling your ex to "see how things are going."

MEALS

Lean Cuisine Pasta Primavera for one, followed by a pint of Häagen-Dazs.

BENEFIT

Save money on costly Valentine's Day gifts—Godiva sampler and long-stem roses.

DRAWBACK

Soul-aching loneliness.

19. *Jeopardy* Loser

THE DAY

Started the game on a $2,000 tear through TV theme songs, then took a nosedive on Art History and Famous Fauna.

DURATION

Twenty-two minutes of fame and a lifetime of regret for answering "Who is Leonardo?" instead of "Who is Michelangelo?"

LOCATION

Sony Studios in Culver City, California.

HAZARD

Loss of winnings, dignity, and even the second-place consolation prize, a ride on a blimp.

BENEFIT

Can be worked into casual conversation on first dates to imply intelligence and invoke pity.

DRAWBACK

Your prize is the home edition of *Jeopardy*. One moment you're playing on national TV, the next you're playing at home against your ten-year-old niece, and she beats you, too.

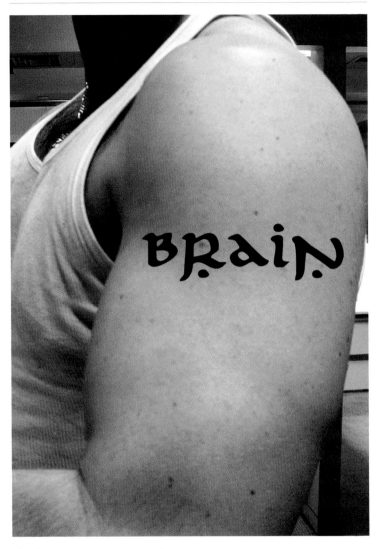

20. Tattoo Typo

THE DAY

Hmm, your name isn't Brain. And you're not that smart, either.

TRAUMA

The new tattoo was really sore for the first two weeks. After that, it's just your pride that hurts.

DURATION

The rest of your life, or until you can afford laser tattoo removal.

BENEFIT

10 percent off for typos.

DRAWBACK

Showering after gym class just got a little more unbearable.

LESSON

Learn to love long sleeves.

21. Bank Hostage

THE DAY

Stopped by your local branch to make a deposit at the same time a robber was making a withdrawal.

DURATION

Varies, depending on how good the hostage negotiator is.

LOCATION

The vault.

TRAUMA

You get Patty Hearst Syndrome, whereby you get brainwashed into helping your captors rob other banks.

BENEFIT

Could get interviewed on the local news.

DRAWBACK

Could get shot.

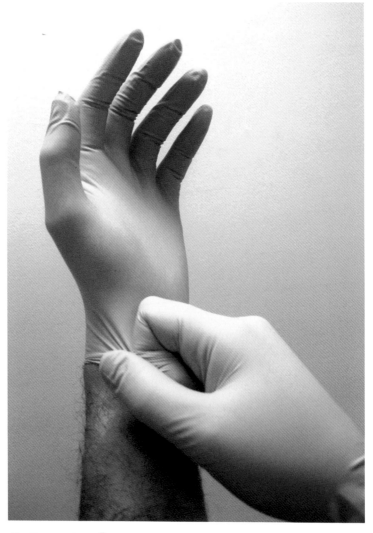

22. Colonoscopy

THE DAY

At some point, we will likely go through this, um, uncomfortable inspection. In addition to *oscopy*, other suffixes to avoid are *itis*, *noma*, and *ectomy*.

LOCATION

Inside. Deep inside.

DURATION

Thirty to sixty minutes.

BENEFIT

They let you keep the video of the procedure—a nice addition to any film collection.

DRAWBACK

Could get interviewed on the local news.

FUN FACT

The Super Colon—an incredible, inflatable, twenty-foot-long, eight-foot-high replica of a human colon—is an interactive educational tool. Every March, the Super Colon goes on a twenty-city national tour. Admission is free.

23. Broke a Nail

THE DAY

All those months forgoing bowling, wasted. Triage includes a silk wrap, Nailtique, nail glue, protein treatments, and cuticle oil.

COST

$5 and a prayer that it works.

TRAUMA

Even if others don't notice, you know you have a fakey.

BENEFIT

No nails makes it easier to finger-scoop peanut butter.

DRAWBACK

Can no longer annoy co-workers by doing that clickity clickity arpeggio on your Formica-top desk.

LESSON

If the nail-enhancing gel doesn't help, a Xanax will.

GRAYCE PEDULLA DILLON

24. Judgment Day

Zephaniah 1:15–17

> "That day will be a day of wrath,
> a day of distress and anguish,
> a day of trouble and ruin,
> a day of darkness and gloom,
> a day of clouds and blackness . . .
> . . . And they will walk like blind men,
> because they have sinned against the LORD.
> Their blood will be poured out like dust
> and their entrails like filth."

Bummer.

Eternity in heaven or eternity in hell. Either way, it's an eternity.

Getting smote by the notorious G-O-D.

Prayer = good. False idols = bad.

Pimple

25. Pimple on Prom Night

THE DAY

As if there isn't enough pressure on prom night—to drink, do drugs, go all the way—now you've got a whitehead on your face that no amount of concealer is going to hide.

LOCATION

Smack in the middle of your face.

WHO SEES

Your parents, your date, and every person who will see the photo on your mantel for years to come.

BENEFIT

Maybe he won't want to go all the way after all.

DRAWBACK

Maybe he won't want to go all the way after all.

LESSON

Skip it. Save the money and go to Jamaica. The prom is overrated. And you know that skank Suzie will win Prom Queen anyway.

26. Forgot Permission Slip

THE DAY

No slip, no trip. Without your parent's signature, the school could be liable, say, if the class trip to the zoo ends in carnage.

WHO SAW

All your classmates as they boarded the bus headed for Hershey Park, the greatest field trip of all time.

LOCATION

Homeroom.

BENEFIT

Eight hours alone in homeroom is ample time to catch up on Civil War history reading.

DRAWBACK

Eight hours alone in homeroom, or as they call it in prison, "a day in the hole," is enough to drive you out of your mind.

LESSON

Forgery. Practice makes perfect.

27. Saturday at the Water Park

THE DAY

Every family in the nine surrounding counties has the same brilliant idea to go to Wet, Wacky 'n' Wild! on the same day.

DURATION

Forty-five-minute line. Forty-five-second slide.

MEALS

Chicken fingers, $11. Small Coke, $4. Eating an over-priced lunch in a wet bathing suit? Priceless.

HAZARD

Seeing your sister-in-law in her bathing suit.

BENEFIT

You've got to admit, the Lagoon Monster Raging Rapids Tube Ride is pretty awesome.

DRAWBACK

E-coli is remarkably resilient against chlorine.

28. Gas Hits $3.19/Gallon

THE DAY

No wonder home schooling is on the rise. No kiddy car-pooling, no driving to parent-teacher conferences: it's the best deal out there.

LOCATION

The pump.

BENEFIT

Gives cantankerous elderly something to complain about besides the weather.

DRAWBACK

Alaskan wildlife better relocate before the U.S. drills into their living rooms.

LESSON

Bicycles aren't just for kids. They're for poor people, too.

FUN FACT

Americans drive more than 2.5 trillion miles per year in automobiles, light trucks, and SUVs—that's equal to 14,000 round trips to the sun!

29. Latte Hits $3.69/Grande

THE DAY

Every day. It's a morning ritual, addiction, and expensive habit all rolled into one.

LOCATION

Your closest Starbucks. Or the one directly across the street. Or the one two blocks up from that one . . .

HAZARD

The summer days are worse. Iced Mocha Frappuccino: $5.20.

BENEFIT

Starbucks is a nice strong brew. According to the Center for Science in the Public Interest, a 16-ounce grande has 550 mg of caffeine; that's the equivalent of 10 cans of Mountain Dew, or 100 smacks in the face.

DRAWBACK

$3.65 per Latte x 365 days a year = $1,332.25. Placing this $100-a-month expenditure into a mutual fund with a conservative 8 percent return will gross you $150,000 in 30 years.

LESSON

Folger's Crystals: 25 cents a cup. Pour it *into* a Starbucks cup and you get into the party without paying admission.

30. Suntan 360°

THE DAY

It seemed like a good idea at the time. Who hasn't wanted an all-over tan?

DURATION

All-day bronzing where the sun shouldn't shine.

LOCATION

Right below the equator.

HAZARD

Minor melanoma and major public embarrassment.

BENEFIT

In certain social circles in Fire Island, the South of France, and the Greek Isles, this is *the* look.

DRAWBACK

Not the right attire for public beaches or anywhere else in public. Or private, for that matter.

31. Team-Building
Field Trip

THE DAY

You and the entire accounting department face a ropes course, the Trust Fall, and the Courage Wall. With teamwork, a company can overcome any obstacle.

DURATION

A group cheer in the morning, seminars during the day, talent show at night.

LOCATION

An old sleepaway camp in the Adirondacks during winter—because hypothermia brings people together.

BENEFIT

It was an employee-bonding experience—Steve and Linda from HR got it on!

DRAWBACK

Having Mike from Shipping grab you by the waist harness and hurl you over the Courage Wall.

TRAUMA

Group showers.

32. When Pigeons Attack

THE DAY

Doves they are not. More like rats with wings. And they are not afraid of you.

WHO SEES

The birds. Every person's head is a target. They perch on lampposts and ledges, just waiting to line you up in the crosshairs.

LOCATION

Your head.

BENEFIT

In some cultures, if a pigeon craps on you, it's good luck.

DRAWBACK

If a pigeon with avian flu does the same, bad luck.

FUN FACT

Pigeons played a vital part in World War I as an extremely reliable way of sending messages. Over 100,000 pigeons were used in the war, with an astonishing success rate of 95 percent getting through to their destinations with their messages. And now they just go on your head, and eat out of the garbage.

33. Wheelie Gone Awry

THE DAY

The sun is out, the birds are chirping, not a cloud in the sky. About the only thing that can crush this ride is an off-duty ambulance driving in reverse.

DURATION

All of three seconds.

WHO SAW

Not the ambulance driver.

BENEFIT

The ambulance is already there.

DRAWBACK

Getting charged with "following too closely" and placed 100 percent at fault for the accident despite nearly being pancaked by the paramedics.

LESSON

It's never good when an ambulance is coming for you.

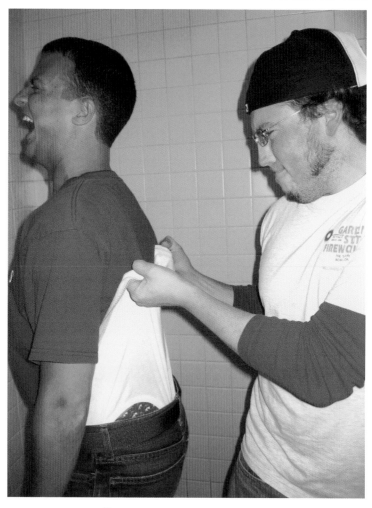

34. Ricky Gets Atomic Wedgie

THE DAY

A wedgie is only atomic if the elastic underwear band makes it up over the unsuspecting victim's head. Ricky knows this well.

WHO SAW

The gym teacher, who, coincidentally, is the basketball coach. And since the wedgie perpetrators were varsity starters, there was no detention for them.

DURATION

A swift few seconds. But the pain will last a lifetime.

BENEFIT

Fueled by rage, Ricky will graduate first in his class, attend Harvard, and make millions.

DRAWBACK

He'll get a wedgie at his twenty-five-year reunion, for old times' sake. And it will be atomic.

LESSON

Going commando never made so much sense.

35. Twenty-One Years and One Day Old

THE DAY

Ah, the day you turn twenty-one. Oh, the morning after.

DURATION

Three Jack and Cokes, four kamikazes, five shots of Patrón tequila, two hours of projectile vomiting, one night in the ER.

WHO SEES

Your closest friends. And, eventually, your parents.

BENEFIT

It's a rite of passage to surrender one's fake ID to the younger sibling. It's the ultimate hand-me-down.

DRAWBACK

The worst bedspins of your life.

LESSON

Make a deal with the bartender in advance to water down your drinks. It's a win-win. The mixologist saves on alcohol, you save on liver.

36. Ate Bad Oyster

THE DAY

To say "I have lived," you must eat certain foods before you die: escargot, something still alive, an entire bucket of KFC, and chilled raw oysters.

DURATION

A two-second slide down the gullet. Followed by twenty-four hours on your knees, praying to the porcelain throne.

BENEFIT

Oysters are a natural aphrodisiac.

DRAWBACK

Vomit is not.

LESSON

Stick to cooked food.

FUN FACT

The Bible commands Jews to stay away from shellfish. Leviticus 11, verses 9–12: "These you may eat of all that are in the water: whatever . . . has fins and scales . . . that you may eat. But in all the seas or in the rivers that do not have fins and scales . . . they are an abomination to you . . . you shall not eat their flesh."

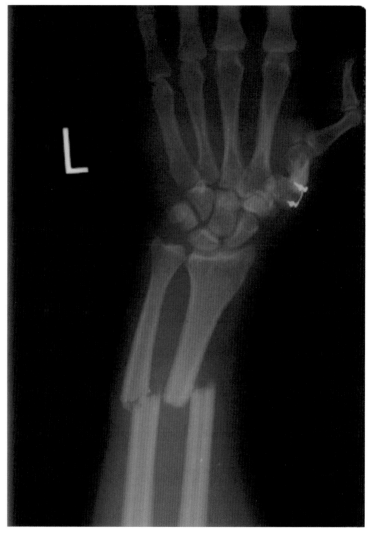

37. Bad Break

THE DAY

Snap. There goes the Ultimate Fighting season.

DURATION

Eight to ten weeks of not being able to scratch that itch under the cast.

HAZARD

Risk factors for forearm fractures: osteoporosis, poor nutrition, and blocking karate kicks.

BENEFIT

Chicks dig scars.

DRAWBACK

"You should see the other guy" seems like too much of a line.

LESSON

Stockpile your Vicodin for a rainy day.

38. New BB Gun

THE DAY

For Christmas, you finally got it. The official Red Ryder carbine-action double-pump air rifle with optional bayonet. You shot your eye out, then fell down and shot your sister's out, too.

WHO SAW

Your little brother, who ratted you out.

DURATION

A lifetime of poor depth perception.

BENEFIT

Your Halloween costume is pretty much picked out for you. Yarrr!

DRAWBACK

It's only cool to be a pirate once a year. Not year round.

LESSON

If you're going to shoot someone in the face, be vice president. (See Hunting with Cheney, no. 3.)

39. Not Enough Snow for a Snow Day

THE DAY

Flurries all night but somehow, in the morning, there's not enough snow to cancel school.

MEALS

The lunch lady has front-wheel drive, so she couldn't make it to school. So if you didn't brown bag it, you're screwed.

HAZARD

Iceball to the eye during recess.

COMMUTE

The "Bataan Death March" trudge through the slush.

BENEFIT

If tonight's snow sticks, school could be canceled tomorrow.

DRAWBACK

The driveway won't shovel itself.

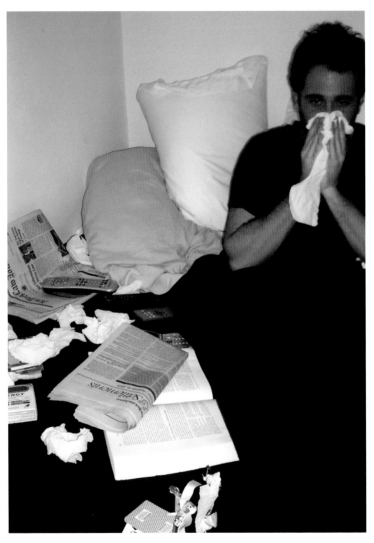

40. Flu, Day 5

THE DAY

Delirious from a 103 fever and loss of fluids, you confuse Bob Barker with God. It's as if Bob/God is welcoming people to spin the wheel of life for a chance to take a first-class trip to that showcase prize package in the sky. You try to eat something, fail, sleep, then *Guiding Light* comes on.

DURATION

There is no clock in hell.

BENEFIT

In the throes of illness, you pledge to be a better person and apologize to all those you've ever hurt before.

DRAWBACK

This is only day 5. Wait until day 7, when even your mother stops taking your calls.

LESSON

Next time, follow Grammy's advice: wear a hat and gloves at all times.

FUN FACT

"80 percent of your body heat exits through the extremities." (Gramma Dinah)

41. Mailed Priceless Stamp

THE DAY

The good grandchild that you are, you decided to write your grandmother a nice little note. Scouring your house for a stamp, you find one in an old desk, and then proceed to mail away the tiny piece of adhesive paper that is worth twenty times the inheritance you'll get out of Granny.

DAMAGE

In mint condition, which the stamp was, it was worth $250,000.

DURATION

It takes the postcard five days to get to your grandmother in Miami Beach, and it takes you the rest of your life to stop kicking yourself.

BENEFIT

Could lead to a fulfilling stamp-collecting hobby.

DRAWBACK

Yearly membership to "Stamp Collector Monthly" is $89/yr. That's just $7.40 an issue. *Just?* That's highway robbery!

LESSON

Look before you lick and stick.

42. Buried

THE DAY

The Blizzard of 2006, three days later.

LOCATION

Tow zone.

DURATION

Two hours in thigh-deep snow.

DAMAGE

A $165 parking ticket and detention boot.

BENEFIT

Major incentive to pay those five outstanding parking tickets.

DRAWBACK

Frostbite and a hernia from hand-scooping snow behind the tires.

43. Mayday, Mayday!

THE DAY

What a clear, beautiful day for a flight or a leisurely hot-air-balloon ride. But not both in the same airspace.

DURATION

Ten hot flaming seconds.

WHO SAW

Everyone at the air show.

BENEFIT

Little Timmy from Arkansas sure got a day to remember.

DRAWBACK

A two-thousand-foot vertical drop.

FUN FACT

Hot-air balloons were invented in France in 1783. Initially balloons without any passengers were sent up. Later, animals of all sorts were used for experimenting, including a sheep, rooster, and duck. (Why bother sending a duck, since it can fly? Who knows. Ask the French.)

44. Ran with the Bulls

THE DAY

Wake up, put on running shoes, do some deep knee bends, run for your life.

LOCATION

Pamplona, until your family can have you medevaced back to the States.

BENEFIT

Come home with a T-shirt that reads "I got horny in Pamplona."

DRAWBACK

Many Pamplonians don't like thrill-seeking tourists. If you try to run and leap out of the street, they will likely push you back in.

LESSON

Angry beef is worse than mad cow.

FUN FACT

The last death occurred in 1995, when twenty-two-year-old Matthew Peter Tassio of Glen Ellyn, Illinois, ran, unsuccessfully, with the bulls.

45. First Day Back at the Gym

THE DAY

You took an *extended* break from the gym. Now you're paying for it.

TRAUMA

Pulls, strains, sprains, tears, pops, and a groin injury.

DURATION

Treadmill: five minutes
Bench Press: two reps
StairMaster: ain't happening.

BENEFIT

You're one pushup closer to optimum beach bod.

DRAWBACK

Before you put on your Speedo, you're going to have to wax that rug off your back.

LESSON

Fifteen minutes in the gym once a year doesn't give you license to eat an entire box of donuts.

46. Rabies Vaccination Day

THE DAY

A leisurely car ride spent with your head out the window turns into your worst nightmare when you arrive at the vet and are injected with a needle full of antibodies.

HAZARD

The veterinarian might decide to check for worms, and he has really cold hands.

DURATION

Only a few seconds, but it stings like almighty.

TRAUMA

Dizziness and nausea. But it's nothing a little toilet water can't fix.

BENEFIT

You won't get "put down" like Old Yeller.

DRAWBACK

A lot of "nice to meet you" derrière sniffing in the vet's waiting area.

47. Nonagenarian
Renews Driver's License

THE DAY

Driving behind (and keeping a safe distance from) Great-Grandpa Dave, going 30 in a 65 zone.

HAZARD

Only his hearing, vision, decreased reaction time, and drowsiness from medications.

BENEFIT

It's one less trip for Meals on Wheels drivers.

DRAWBACK

Cataracts in a Cadillac. His blind spot is pretty much everywhere.

LESSON

Don't drive in Florida or Arizona.

FUN FACT

Within twenty years, by one economist's estimate, there will be more crash fatalities involving elderly drivers than there are drunk-driving fatalities (15,935) today. And drunken elderly drivers really don't stand a chance.

48. Fastball in the Nuts

THE DAY

The pitcher looks for the sign, nods, winds up, pumps, and fires a heater right into Jose's chimichangas.

DURATION

Replayed over and over on Sports Center and then immortalized on *Wacky Sports Bloopers Volume 8*.

COMMUTE

It's only ninety feet to first base, but ninety feet feels like a marathon when you're doubled over and crying.

BENEFIT

Improves his on-base percentage. And perhaps a future career as an opera soprano.

DRAWBACK

Say adios to any hopes of a Jose Jr.

TRAUMA

Jose will never take an inside pitch again.

49. Thanksgiving at the In-laws'

THE DAY

You spend $400 on an airplane ticket to take a vacation that is anything but. Your girlfriend's siblings hate you. To date, the dog has bitten you four times. Forty-eight hours that seem like a lifetime.

LOCATION

Dante's Fourth Circle of Hell.

FUN FACT

After three years of going out with their *baby* they still make you sleep in separate bedrooms. Actually, you're bunking with grandpapa.

BENEFIT

If your future brother in-law, the alcoholic gambler, comes, you're not public enemy number one.

DRAWBACK

The turkey is dry, the giblets are super chunky. You have to eat three portions to be polite.

LESSON

Next holiday, elope for Thanksgiving.

50. Your Last Day

THE DAY

You kicked it, cashed in the chips, bought the farm, got called up to the big league in the sky.

LOCATION

Nine to five, Earth. Five to forever, Heaven.

DURATION

About thirty minutes through the light. There was a little traffic in purgatory.

BENEFIT

No more Blockbuster late fees, ever.

DRAWBACK

There's a vicious rumor that there's no Starbucks up there. And down there—only decaf.

LESSON

Eat more lettuce. But not iceberg. Iceberg is mostly water with few nutrients. Choose romaine. Or mesclun.

51. Your Day

THE DAY

LOCATION

DURATION

BENEFIT

DRAWBACK

LESSON

PHOTOGRAPHERS

Adam and Eve Eat Apple: *The Rebuke of Adam and Eve* by Domenichino
Bris: Paul Van Metre
Hunting with Cheney: Billy Siegrist Photography
SATs: Mareen Fischinger http://fotografischinger.de
Saturday A.M. Violin Practice: Gemma Choi
Shark Bite: Carl Roessler, copyright 2003, Department of Defense
Lost the Spelling Bee: Justin Rudd
Bridesmaid, Yet Again: Julie Soefer
Not This Dog's Day: Scott Frankel
Jury Duty: Daniel Berman
Ousted from Clique: Tina Ritter
Judgment Day: *Waiting for the Son*, Grayce Pedulla Dillon
Pimple on Prom Night: Mr. Passaro
Forgot Permission Slip: Amy Benati
Saturday at the Water Park: Brandy Hollins
Gas Hits $3.19/Gallon: Jim Olsen
Latte Hits $3.69/Grande: Julie Soefer
Suntan 360: Pete
When Pigeons Attack: Nic Bannon
Wheelie Gone Awry: Mark Rabo Photography
Twenty-one Years and One Day Old: Mark Rabo
Ate Bad Oyster: Art Siegel
New BB Gun: Mary Kay Mann
Not Enough Snow for a Snow Day: Elisa Resnik
Mailed Priceless Stamp: James Redekop & Lori Welland
Mayday, Mayday!: Laura Jane, Chris Nielson
Ran with the Bulls: Yi Liu
Fastball in the Nuts: Michael Schipper
Thanksgiving at the In-laws': Richard Giles
Your Last Day: Ann Sanfredel, *Sign Language: A Photograph Album of Visual Puns* (Citadel Press, 1992)

All others photographed by Justin Racz and Alec Brownstein.
Retouching: Zach Hirsh, Eric Van Skyhawk, Julie Soefer
Cartoons: Daniel Berman
Icon illustrations: Laurel Tynsdale